CAMP
COOKING

CAMP
COOKING

15×1|07 ✓ 7|07

Bill and Jo McMorris

The Lyons Press

Illustrations by Ron Butler

Printed in the United States of America

Library of Congress Cataloging-in-Publication Data

McMorris, Bill.
      Camp cooking.

      Includes index.
      1. Outdoor cookery. 2. Backpacking. I. McMorris, Jo. II. Title.
TX823M37 1988   641.5'782   88-27184
ISBN 1-55821-023-7

CAMP
COOKING

Contents

Introduction

*W*eight is serious business to backpackers. So is flavor in the food they carry. The purpose of this book is to help long distance hikers fill small, light packages with nourishing food that can be turned into tasty meals over a campfire or one-burner stove.

Small stoves, portable grates and compact utensils are some of the self-imposed restrictions of the backpacker. Limited food supplies are also part of the proposition. But as food technology creates ever lighter and more appealing dishes, trail menus are less confining. To those who have never known the freedom of roaming the wilderness with a backpack, such restrictions may seem like hardships. But backpackers accept these limitations gladly.

Those who have paid the price to travel light and free know that the rewards are great: The sight of a stream of painted-lady butterflies migrating along a snowy shoulder of Mt. Rainier; the ghostly curtains of the Northern Lights above an island campsite in Canada; evening flights of white herons in the Florida Everglades; the misty silence of an autumn morning in the Endless Mountains of Pennsylvania; the clatter of a Bighorn Sheep traversing a talus slope in the Arizona desert; these and a thousand other small meetings with the natural world are what a backpacker earns.

Best of all these experiences may be the shared warmth of good food and friendship on the trail. To that experience, especially, this book is directed.

▲▲

Fire, Water and Utensils

*T*houghts of cooking outdoors usually bring with them a picture of pots steaming over a glowing wood fire, warming the heart as well as the meal. Unfortunately, it's a scene that has to become less common as use of the back-country increases.

Campfires are delightful, but they also offer serious drawbacks. They are hard to start and keep burning in wet weather. As a heat source for cooking they are difficult to control. They scar the ground, and can create a fire hazard, especially in dry brush and timber. In some well travelled areas, the ground has been scoured bare of fallen limbs, tempting campers to strip standing trees of dead and not-so-dead branches. For these reasons open fires are often banned in many national parks and wilderness areas. If you are determined to cook over an open fire, be sure to check regulations before you set out on the trail.

The very nature of backpacking may also rule out open fires. When you camp above timberline or in some desert regions and along many beaches, proper wood for a cookfire may be difficult or impossible to find.

A good single-burner stove increases a backpacker's freedom and provides a cookfire that is easy to light and control. And it doesn't blacken pots.

A one-burner stove will handle cooking needs for four campers, but a second stove is worth the extra weight for the speed and convenience it will add in preparing meals for a party of that size.

No matter what kind of fire you use for cooking, make sure you take along plenty of wooden matches, some of them in a waterproof container.

STOVE FUELS

A good fuel for a backpacking stove lights quickly, burns with a clean, hot flame, and doesn't add too much weight to a pack. It should burn well at any altitude in any weather and be easy to obtain.

Gasoline: Unleaded "white" gasoline made for camping may be the best all-around fuel for the trail. It is widely available, burns hot regardless of altitude or air temperature, and, unlike automotive fuel, does not clog stoves or soot-up pots. It can be carried in light, reusable containers.

Disadvantages: Very flammable if spilled or handled carelessly around open flames. Fuel leaks can ruin food.

Kerosene: Burns about as hot as gasoline in all conditions and is somewhat safer to use. It is not as easy to find in the United States as it once was, but it is often used in foreign countries. Kerosene fuel containers can be refilled.

Disadvantages: It is harder to light than gasoline. It evaporates slowly if spilled. Kerosene has a strong, long-lasting odor. Leaks can spoil food, and it must be handled carefully to avoid accidental fires.

Propane and Butane: As easy to light as a gas range at home. Gas stored in cannisters under pressure furnishes an instant, clean flame that does not have an odor or blacken pots.

Disadvantages: Performs poorly in cold temperatures. Heavier and more costly than liquid fuels and does not burn as hot as liquid fuels. A gas cannister usually cannot be removed from the stove until it is empty. It is impossible to tell how much fuel remains in the cannister. Empty containers must be packed out of the wilderness.

Alcohol: The least useful fuel for the backpacker's stove. It may be used in its safe, solid form (such as Sterno) occasionally to heat a cup or two of hot water, but it is not practical for cooking. Sometimes it is carried to use as a primer for stoves using other liquid fuels.

BACKPACKING STOVES

A good stove should burn hot, be reliable, easy to light and adjust, furnish a firm base for a cooking pot and be equipped with some kind of wind screen. Light weight and ease of maintenance are other important virtues.

Never attempt to fill any liquid fuel stove while it is burning or while the stove is hot. Follow carefully the manufacturer's instructions for use. Adult supervision is recommended when young people use any camp stove.

Coleman Peak 1 White Gas Stove: This stove is easy to light and gives a strong, hot flame very quickly. It makes a firm base for pots and has a 10 oz. fuel tank that will serve most small parties through a long weekend. It has a built-in pressure pump, wind screen and cleaning needle. With fuel it weighs about 2.5 pounds.

Coleman Peak 1 Multi-fuel Stove: By switching vaporizers you convert this stove from white gas to kerosene. It has a slightly smaller fuel tank than the Peak 1, but otherwise it has all the same virtues and weighs about 12 ozs. less with a full tank of fuel.

MSR WhisperLite Stove: This Mountain Safety Research product lights fast and burns hot under all conditions with white gas from an aluminum fuel tank. The tank, purchased separately, is pressurized with a pump from the stove. Tanks come in several sizes, from about 10 ozs. to more than a quart. A windscreen and reflector are built into the stove. The stove weighs a little over 13 ozs. (without fuel) and folds to fit into a cook kit.

MSR also has a model called the X-GK that can burn various kinds of gasoline, kerosene, solvent, diesel fuel and stove oil. Hikers in remote parts of the world would find it especially useful.

Optimus 8R: This Optimus burns white gas, is compact and weighs only 1 lb. 10 ozs. with 4 ozs. of fuel. The stove's metal case forms a wind screen. It must be primed by burning some fuel or alcohol in a small cup at the bottom of the burner stem before the fuel in the tank will vaporize and burn properly. It may be fussy in extremely cold weather, but this can be offset by use of an Optimus Mini-Pump (purchased separately) to pressurize the tank. Pots will be somewhat less stable than on other models mentioned.

Other Optimus models burn kerosene alone or a variety of fuels.

Bleuet: The butane gas in the C-206 cartridge lights instantly in mild temperatures and burns full blast for more than three hours, but it puts out less heat than white gas and kerosene. In freezing weather at sea level the cartridge must be kept above 30 degrees if it is to burn at all. (At higher altitudes it will function at colder temperatures because of reduced air pressure.) The base is too narrow and the stove too tall for good stability. The cartridge must not be removed until the butane is exhausted. With a full cartridge the stove weighs 1 lb. 6 ozs. Empty cartridges weigh 3.3 ozs. apiece and must be packed out of the wilderness.

Svea 123R: Very light, at 1 lb., 8 ozs. with 6 ozs. of white gas. A built-in wind screen and a small pot and pot lifter are part of the package. It burns hot but requires priming. Like

the Optimus 8R, it needs pressurizing in cold weather and the same Optimus Mini-Pump may be used. It does not offer as stable a platform as some other models. A stripped down model of this stove fits into a cook kit and wind screen designed for it. (A description of the cook kit appears later in this chapter.)

UTENSILS

All recipes in this book are planned for a party of four. All the recipes can be cooked quite easily in the compact, nesting cook kits designed for backpackers.

Sigg, a Swiss company, has for many years specialized in cook kits of stainless steel designed to work with single-burner stoves. One model can hold the WhisperLite or Bleuet stoves, while others are intended to contain

Peak 1 or Svea 123 stoves. The Svea version encloses a stripped-down stove and acts as a stove base and wind screen as well as a cook kit. All these kits include 2½-pint and 3½-pint pots, a pot lifter and a lid that serves as a 7¾–inch skillet.

The stainless steel kits weigh between 1 pound, 4 oz. and almost 2 lbs. They are sturdy, well finished and long-lasting and do not leave metal streaks on rocks where they are used.

Aluminum kits with three or four larger pots and lid-skillets are also available at about the same weight as the smaller stainless-steel kits. Larger pots (up to 3½ qts.) will handle double and even triple recipes. The size of the party will determine the capacity of the cook kit and the number of stoves needed for efficient cooking.

Whatever the choice of stove and group cooking pots, each hiker should carry a personal cup, bowl and pan along with a fork and spoon. It's possible to get by with just a large metal cup and a spoon, but by the time you have had courses of soup, beef stroganoff, pudding and coffee from the same cup, the coffee may taste odd and look worse.

A long-handled spoon and a spatula are the only utensils needed to prepare these backpacker's recipes. These items should be light-

weight and made of metal so they can be sterilized over flame before each meal. A sharp, thin-bladed knife may also be useful for filleting any fish taken on the trip. For anyone willing to carry a few extra ounces, a wire whisk blends freeze-dried eggs, pancake batter, gravies and soups better than any spoon. A set of plastic measuring spoons and a plastic measuring cup are also helpful. Most hikers will have a knife equipped with a can opener, but you may want to carry a separate can opener also.

Two pieces of denim or other durable cloth may be sewn together to create four or five narrow pockets to hold the cooking tools. This "cook's caddy" can be rolled compactly.

WATER

Safe water is essential to cooking and to a happy trip. Unfortunately, pollution has found its way into streams and lakes once considered remote.

Giardia lamblia parasites carried by animals have been found even in high mountain streams. These tiny protozoa can cause painful intestinal upset. There is *only one sure way* to get rid of them: Boil all drinking and cooking water for at least ten minutes. In some recipes, cooking time is long enough to do the job.

Giardia are sometimes large enough to be filtered by some rather slow and expensive devices, but filtration has not proved to be effective in every case.

Water purification tablets also kill germs, but they aren't totally dependable and they give the water a disagreeable iodine or chlorine taste and smell. (If you decide to use purification pills, beverage recipes in Chapter 2 suggest ways to disguise this taste.) Follow the directions for tablet use exactly. Tablets take at least twenty minutes to be effective.

Muddy water should be allowed to stand until particles settle. Clear water can be scooped from the top of the container and boiled or otherwise treated. Straining cloudy water through a clean cloth will eliminate large organic material.

Collapsible plastic water carriers in 2½- and 5-gallon sizes are useful to store large amounts of water at the campsite. The containers can be emptied and carried to the next site when the party is ready to move on.

Chemical contamination will not be removed by filters, tablets or boiling. In areas where chemical pollution is a possibility, prior information from state or local government agencies is your only defense.

CLEAN UP

Cleaning up starts with personal cleanliness. Always wash your hands before preparing food and eating. After meals, scrub out personal dishes and pots with forest litter or sand and rinse with clear water well away from the campsite and from any water source. Pots that are especially sticky can be soaked in cold water before wiping and rinsing. Before the next meal, the utensils can be dipped in boiling water to sanitize them. Metal implements can be sterilized over an open flame.

Many campers prefer not to use soap in the cleanup process because a small amount of soap in the common food supply can inflict diarrhea on an entire group. If you feel you must use soap, choose one of the biodegradable soaps in liquid form. They clean well in cold water and can be spread on the outsides of pots to ease the chore of soot removal should the pots be used on a campfire. Soapy water must be dumped far from the campsite and from any water source.

If you are allowed to have an open fire, burn all cans and foil wrappers, smash cans flat and pack them in a garbage bag to carry out. If you can't burn the cans and other long-lasting trash, clean them up, mash them and pack them out in a tightly closed bag. Secure trash items that carry food odors just as you would protect your food supply to avoid unwelcome wild visitors.

The cardinal rule of cleanup in the wilderness is to pack out every piece of trash you bring in. Scout groups and others interested in conservation of the natural scene go a step further. They carry out all they bring in plus trash they find along the way.

▲▲

Take-along Foods You Make at Home

*B*efore you leave the comfort and convenience of your own kitchen, there's a lot you can do to get your trail supplies prepared. Baking, packaging and mixing at home will make your life much easier on the evening you arrive late at your campsite pursued by darkness and hunger.

TRAIL BREADS

Hearty, rich and satisfying, trail breads are almost a meal by themselves. Add peanut butter, honey or jam and they are a complete lunch. Breads can be frozen until you are ready to depart. Keep the slices tightly wrapped until they are served.

TRAPPER'S OAT BREAD

Yield: 8 5-oz. trail slices
Keeps for two weeks in mild weather.

1 cup unbleached white flour
3½ cups oatmeal
½ cup dry milk powder
½ cup honey
1 cup butter or margarine, softened
1 egg, slightly beaten
⅔ cup raisins
½ cup chopped dates*
½ cup sliced almonds, pecan chips or chopped
  walnuts
shortening

Cream together the margarine and honey.
Add the slightly beaten egg and blend well.

Mix the flour, oatmeal, and dry milk in a
large mixing bowl and sift the mixture with
your hands until ingredients are well com-
bined.

Add the dry ingredients to the margarine,
honey and egg mixture. Mix well, then add
the raisins, dates and nuts. Stir well.

Using a good load of shortening on a paper
towel, grease a 9 × 13 × 2-inch cake pan.

*Chopped dates are available in packages at your grocery
store. They are dusted with sugar before packaging in
order to keep them from sticking together. If you don't
want the extra sugar, chop your own dates.

Spread the batter into the pan. Bake at 300 degrees for 45 to 50 minutes. The bread will be a warm bronze color when done.

Cut the bread into 8 trail slices. Let the slices cool slightly, then remove them from the pan. Allow the bread to dry on a baker's rack for 15 to 20 minutes before wrapping in plastic or foil. A slice of this bread spread with honey or peanut butter is a filling lunch on the trail. A half-slice makes a good dessert at the evening meal.

BEST GUIDE'S BREAD

Yield: 16 4-oz. trail slices
Keeps for two weeks in mild weather.

6 cups unbleached white flour
1 cup wheat bran
1½ cups brown sugar
1 cup dry milk powder
2 teaspoons salt
2 cups water
1 cup honey
1 cup safflower oil
2½ cups raisins
1 cup nuts (pecan chips, walnut pieces or
   sliced almonds)
1 cup chopped dates

Put the flour, bran, sugar, dry milk, and salt in a large mixing bowl and sift the mixture with your fingers until the ingredients are well blended. Combine the water, honey and oil; add this mixture to the dry ingredients. Stir well. Add the raisins, dates and nuts to the batter, stirring well to distribute the fruit evenly.

Grease two 9 × 13 × 2-inch cake pans. Divide the batter equally between the two pans and bake in a 300-degree oven for 1 hour. Let the bread cool slightly, then cut into 16 slices. Air dry the bread on a baker's rack for 15 or 20 minutes before wrapping in plastic or foil.

BRAN NUT MUFFINS

Yield: 18 large 2-oz. muffins
Keeps ten days in mild weather

1½ cups boiling water
1 cup raisins
½ cup chopped dates
⅔ cup brown sugar
2 tablespoons safflower oil
1 egg, slightly beaten
2 cups unbleached white flour
1 teaspoon salt
1 teaspoon baking soda
2 teaspoons cinnamon
1½ cups wheat bran
⅔ cup chopped walnuts

Pour the boiling water over the raisins and date pieces in a small bowl. Let the mix cool to lukewarm.

Add the brown sugar, oil and egg to the water and fruit.

Put the flour, salt, soda, cinnamon and bran in a large mixing bowl and sift the combination with your fingers. Combine the dry ingredients with the liquid mixture. Mix well, add the nuts and fill well-greased muffin tins with the batter. Fill each muffin cup about ¾ full. Bake for 20–25 minutes in a 400-degree oven.

Allow the muffins to cool slightly, then remove from the pan. Wrap the muffins in foil or plastic. These muffins freeze well, but will keep fresh for ten days without refrigeration.

TRAIL MIXES FOR BREAKFAST AND SNACKS

Granola for breakfast and trail mix for munching on the trail offer nutrition and good flavor.

BLOATED OATIES

Yield: 10 half-cup servings

3 cups instant rolled oats
¼ cup safflower oil
½ cup wheat germ
½ cup pecan chips, sliced almonds or chopped walnuts
½ cup dried apples, chopped or grated
½ cup raisins
¼ cup brown sugar

Spread the oats on a cookie sheet and drizzle the oil over them. Place the oats in a 300-degree oven for ten minutes, stirring occasionally to blend the oats and oil. Remove the oats and let cool.

Place the oats in a large mixing bowl and add the wheat germ and brown sugar. Stir to blend and add the nuts, apples and raisins.

Divide the oaties into half-cup servings and pack them in individual self-sealing plastic bags.

To serve, add 2 tablespoons of dry milk powder and ⅔ cup of purified water to the granola mix. To serve this cereal hot, add a dash of salt to the dry mix before adding boiling water.

TRAIL MIX

Yield: 15 cups (with one optional item)

2 cups honey roast cashew nuts
2 cups dry roasted peanuts
2 cups pecan pieces (8 oz. package)
2 cups mixed nuts (11 oz. can)
2 cups fruit bits (prepackaged dried fruits, 6 oz. package)
2 cups raisins
1 cup sunflower kernels

Options to add, determined by preference: 2 cups candy-coated chocolate bits

or

½ cup chopped dates
1 cup golden sultana raisins
½ cup whole almonds

or

1 cup freeze-dried pineapple
½ cup coconut
½ cup freeze-dried banana chips

or

2 cups roasted, salted cashews

Combine the ingredients, adding the options of your choice. Bag in self-sealing plastic sandwich bags.

Drink Mixes

Prepackaged and re-packaged to save time and weight on the trail, they help to hide the taste of water purification tablets.

Coffee & Tea

Coffee is a favorite hot beverage of many hikers. If you and your hiking companions are coffee lovers, you may prefer to take along ground coffee to add to boiling water. Simply add one tablespoon of ground coffee for every

8- ounce cup of boiling water and add an extra tablespoon "for the pot." The coffee can be carried in a plastic bag. Instant coffee can be repacked in a plastic bag. Follow the manufacturer's directions to mix. Tea bags are available in many varieties. English Breakfast Tea is strong and full-bodied enough to start anyone's day. Many herb teas are available in bags, as well. Any of the tea bags can be carried in plastic bags.

LEMON SPICE TEA

½ cup instant 100% tea
1 .31-oz. package of unsweetened lemon soft
   drink mix
4 tablespoons sugar or equivalent sweetener
One-inch piece of cinnamon

Put all the ingredients in a plastic zippered bag along with a plastic teaspoon for measuring. On the trail, stir one teaspoon tea mix (not cinnamon) into 8 ounces hot or cold water.*

ORANGE AND CLOVE TEA

½ cup instant 100% tea
¼ cup Tang drink mix
2 tablespoons sugar or equivalent sweetener
4 whole cloves

*See Chapter 1 for suggestions on water purification.

Place all the ingredients in a plastic zippered bag. Include a plastic teaspoon for measuring. Mix 2 teaspoons tea blend (no cloves) with 6 ounces hot or cold water.

Other Beverages

Fruit flavored, pre-sweetened drink powders offer the hiker refreshment on the trail or after the day's trek.

Strawberry, orange, lemon and chocolate drinks are available in boxes of individual packets on your grocer's shelves. Remove the envelopes from the boxes they are sold in and put them in re-sealable plastic bags. A strip of masking tape with directions for mixing written in indelible marker will help you in on-the-trail preparation.

Powdered dry milk can be stored in sturdy plastic re-sealable bags. A ⅓-cup measuring cup can be packed in the milk bag. To mix 1 cup of milk, add ⅓-cup of the milk powder to a 7 or 8 ounce cup of purified water.

Seasonings, Shortenings & Condiments

Salt, pepper, mayonnaise, mustard, and relish are available at wholesale food stores in individual serving sizes. Check with your local grocer if you do not have such a store in your area.

Pack all your seasonings and condiments in one large, freezer-weight zippered plastic bag, and mark it with a colorful sticker or piece of colored tape for easy identification. In addition to the items listed above, include at least a quarter pound of shortening in a plastic bag. The most convenient variety for backpackers is packaged as four ¼-pound sticks to a box. This vegetable shortening requires no refrigeration.

Many campers, hiking in the high country, like to include margarine in their "pantry." Probably the easiest form of butter substitute spread is the variety packaged in a squeeze bottle.

Seasoning salt can be found on your grocer's shelf. A dash of this flavorful substance will work wonders on packaged soup mixes and one-dish meals. Simply pour the seasoning salt into a freezer weight zippered plastic bag. Two ounces will be enough to carry for a 4–5 day trip.

Two items which will add spice and flavor to your trail meals, and weigh only a few ounces are 1) a plastic bag of herbs and spice mix and 2) a few packets of butter buds. The latter item can be found at your grocery. The "buds" are natural butter-flavor granules packaged in ½-ounce packets and sold in boxes of eight packets per box. This product can be sprinkled dry over the noodle, rice and potato recipes in this book. The granules also can be sprinkled over scrambled eggs or added to soups and gravies.

The spice mixture can be blended at home using spices and herbs from your spice cabinet or purchased ready-mixed from your grocer. In either case, you will want to pack the mixture in a sandwich-size resealable plastic bag.

HERB MIX

1 teaspoon oregano
1 teaspoon basil
1 teaspoon sesame seeds
½ teaspoon crushed thyme
½ teaspoon crushed
**   rosemary**
dash of garlic powder

Combine all the ingredients in a sandwich size plastic bag. Seal the bag and shake to mingle the herbs. Use sparingly in instant soups and main dish meals.

Other Items to Add Flavor to Your Trail Meal

An option which you may want to consider is a tube of tomato paste. This tomato concentrate enhances any of the canned beef meals and can be used with salt, pepper and the herb mix in hot water for a quick soup.

Tubes of tomato paste are available from:

Williams Sonoma, Inc.
P.O. Box 7456
San Francisco, CA. 94120-7456

Peanut butter, a perennial favorite of backpackers, can be packaged in freezer-weight resealable plastic bags.

Jelly can be put in lightweight plastic squeeze containers. Allow about one cup per person for a five-day jaunt. Honey can be found at the grocery already packaged in squeeze bottles of 6 or 12 ounces.

Crackers & Crispbreads

Wasa Hearty Rye Crispbread and Sesame Crispbread are good crackers for the camper. They are thick rectangles of fiber that take very well to peanut butter, canned cheese or deviled ham or chicken. They weigh very little and will go well with a bowl of soup or a plate of scrambled eggs.

Pasta and Rice to Add to Packaged Meals

An 8-ounce package of ½-inch (medium) width noodles and a 7-ounce box of instant rice will enable you to increase the quantities of the one dish recipes in Chapter 6. By adding 1 cup of noodles or ½ cup of instant rice to the foil-packed dinners, you will increase each serving by ⅔ cup. Due to the addition of gravies indicated in the recipes there will be no dilution of flavor.

Simple Desserts

A variety of flavors of instant puddings are available and can be mixed on the trail with a minimum of effort. Remove the envelopes from the boxes and put them in plastic bags. Write the directions for mixing on a strip of masking tape and stick it on the bag. Combine the mix with dry milk powder and clean water on the trail.

Cheesecake mixes can be divided and will provide dessert for two meals. A piece of the Best Guide's Bread can be crumbled for the crust. As there are recipes for pie-pan breads included in Chapter 3, an aluminum pie pan or two are handy additions to the trail kitchen and add very little weight. Use one of the pie pans for your cheesecake. Top the cheesecake with wild blueberries if you can find them.

Food From Nature

Fishing tackle and a license may help you add to your food supply. You will need some flour or cornmeal to coat the catch before frying. The shortening referred to earlier in this chapter is ideal for your fish fry. If you plan on catching fish, increase the amount of the shortening you carry.

If you are going to be hiking in blueberry country, take a small bag of cinnamon-sugar mix along to sweeten and spice any berries you find. Four tablespoons of sugar and a scant ¼ teaspoon of cinnamon will be sufficient for a five-day hike.

Wild mushrooms can enhance a meal also, but leave them alone unless you are experienced in finding the safe varieties. Some can sicken you, others can kill.

▲▲▲

3

Breads on The Trail

*I*n addition to the trail breads you bake at home to take along, you will want some lighter, hot breads for variety. The following recipes can be baked in aluminum pie pans on top of your single burner stove. We call them "Clothes Pin Breads" because the stove-top oven they are baked in is made by securing two aluminum pie pans together with snap-style clothespins.

CLOTHES PIN BISCUIT RING

1½ cups Bisquick or other instant biscuit mix
⅓ cup cold water
2 8-inch aluminum pie pans
3 or 4 snap-style wooden clothes pins, soaked in water
5–6 tablespoons vegetable shortening

In a small cookpot or a plastic bowl, mix the Bisquick and the water with a fork until the combination is well blended and sticky. Put two to three tablespoons of vegetable shortening in one of the pans and place it on your stove to melt. Grease the other pie pan thoroughly. Spread the biscuit dough around the outer edge of the pan of melted shortening, leaving the center clear. Put the other pan on top of the dough. Line up the edges of the pie pans and fasten the pans together with the clothespins. Establish a steady, low flame on your stove, and put the biscuit-filled pans on the burner to bake. Bake the bread about 4 minutes on one side, then invert the pan-oven and cook the second side for another 4–5 minutes. Continue to bake the bread another 6–8 minutes, alternating the sides every 2 to 3 minutes. You can take the pan off the stove to check for doneness. If the bread is still soft in the center, continue to cook, alternating sides for another 3–4 minutes. Cut the bread into wedges and serve with margarine, honey or jam.

BLUEBERRY BREAD

1 7-oz. package blueberry muffin mix
4 tablespoons dry milk powder
½ cup cold water
2 8-inch aluminum pie pans
3–4 wooden snap style clothespins, soaked in water
4–6 tablespoons vegetable shortening

Grease the two pie pans well with the shortening. Set the camp stove burner to a steady low flame and put one of the pans on the burner to melt the shortening. Combine the muffin mix, dry milk powder and cold water. Stir just until blended. The batter will be lumpy. Spoon the dough into the pie pan which has been pre-heated. Spread the dough evenly around the outer edge of the pan and top with the second greased pie pan. Secure the edges of the pans with the clothespins which have been soaked in water to prevent burning. Bake for 4 to 5 minutes on one side, then invert the pie-pan oven and continue to bake for another 5 minutes. Alternate the pan sides for another 4 minutes until the bread is done. Cut into wedges and serve.

SKILLET BREADS

A bannock-style bread can be baked in a skillet like a big pancake. To serve, simply cut the mound of bread into wedges.

1¾ cups Bisquick or other biscuit mix, plus an
    additional 2–4 tablespoons to coat the hands
½ cup cold water
3–4 tablespoons oil, margarine or vegetable
    shortening

Light the stove and establish a steady, low flame. In a small aluminum skillet, melt the shortening. Mix the biscuit mix and water together with a fork until the ingredients are well blended and the mixture is sticky. Coat your hands with some of the biscuit mix and pat the dough into a soft ball. Place the ball of dough into the skillet and gently press down with a spatula or pancake turner. Cook the mound of dough until it starts to brown and get dry. Turn the dough and continue to cook until the second side is brown. Serve in wedges with any of the main dinner courses or for breakfast on layover days.

POTATO PATTIES

Although potatoes are a vegetable, these fried patties can be used as a bread substitute.

1 2-oz. package mashed potatoes
1½ cups cold water
⅓ cup dry milk powder
1 tablespoon butter buds or 2 tablespoons
  margarine
salt or seasoning salt to taste
2–3 tablespoons vegetable shortening

Measure the water into a saucepan and add the dry milk powder. Stir to blend, then add the butter buds or the margarine. Bring this mixture to a boil, add about ¼ teaspoon of salt, and the contents of the mashed potato package. Stir gently until the potato flakes are soft and moist. Melt the vegetable shortening in a skillet over medium heat. When the grease is hot, fry the potato patties using about three tablespoons potato batter per patty. Cook until brown on one side, turn and brown the second side. This recipe will make 6 patties.

CORNCAKES

Cornbread mixes can be used for corncakes by adding an additional 2 tablespoons of water to the mix. There seems to be no substitute for the fresh eggs necessary to make these cakes really tasty. We have tried freeze-dried eggs, which produce a gritty texture. Powdered eggs will work but they are difficult to find in grocery stores and wholesale markets. If you plan to carry eggs with you on your short backpack trips, include a package of cornbread mix, follow the directions on the package and bake as directed for Potato Patties.

▲▲

4

Breakfasts and Beverages

*T*rail breakfasts come in two varieties: quick and easy for those mornings you want to hit the trail early, and slow and easy for lay-over mornings.

Either meal calls for something to drink. Whether you prefer a hot or cold beverage, the items listed in Chapter 2 will give you some ideas.

Water should be boiled the night before so you will have a cool, clean supply to mix with your fruit-flavored powders.

BACON AND EGGS

2 2.2-oz foil packages of freeze-dried scrambled
   egg mix
2 cups cold water
2 tablespoons margarine
3 oz 100% Real Bacon Bits*

Cook the eggs as directed on the packages.
Sprinkle with the bacon bits when the eggs
are cooked to the desired consistency. These
eggs do not taste like fresh eggs. It is best to
think of these as scrambled protein. Serve
with Hearty Wasa Rye Crispbread or one of
the skillet or clothes pin breads from Chapter
3. Makes four 1¾ egg servings.

*This product by George A. Hormel & Co., can be trans-
ferred from its original container to a resealable, air-tight
plastic bag. Although the label on the package recom-
mends refrigerating after the package is opened, the
bacon will retain its freshness without refrigeration for up
to two weeks if moisture is kept out of the bacon.

HAM AND POTATO PATTIES

1 package Bordens Country Store mashed
  potatoes (2-oz. size)
1½ cups water
1 tablespoon Butter Buds
3 tablespoons dry milk powder
1 6¾-oz. can chunked ham
2 tablespoons margarine
Seasoning salt and pepper to taste

Mix the milk powder in ½ cup of cold water.
Bring 1 cup of water and the butter buds to a
boil in a small saucepan over high heat. Remove from the heat and add the ½ cup of
milk. Blend well. Add the entire package of
potato flakes and stir until the flakes are absorbed and the mixture is smooth and moist.
Beat briskly with a fork and set aside. Open
the can of ham. Put the margarine in a frying
pan and melt it over a medium flame. Flake
the ham and add a half of the can to the
melted margarine. Fry briefly to heat the ham
through and get it crispy. Portion the meat in
the pan into 4 piles and top each portion of
ham with 2 tablespoons of mashed potatoes.
Press the potato and ham into patties. Adjust
your stove to a steady low flame and fry the
patties until they are browned, about 2 minutes. Brown the other side. Sprinkle with sea-

soning salt and pepper to taste. The ham will add some salt to the patties, so use the seasoning salt sparingly. When the first batch of patties are cooked, repeat the process with the remainder of the ham and the potatoes. Serve with a fruit drink, a hot beverage and some Hearty Wasa Rye for a breakfast that will hold you until lunch.

PANCAKE ROLLUPS

These thin crepe-like pancakes cook in a jiffy and can be rolled up to eat with fingers, or served on a plate and eaten with a fork. For variety, fill some with shredded ham and end the meal with rollups dipped in honey.

> 1½ cups complete pancake mix
> 1½ cups water
> 1 teaspoon sugar
> solid shortening to grease the skillet
> 1 6¾-oz. can chunked ham
> honey or jelly

Combine the pancake mix and the water. Note that these are in equal amounts so if you and your party cannot eat 6 rollups each, cut the recipe to 1 cup each of water and pancake mix. Add the sugar and stir with a wire whisk until the mixture is smooth. Pre-heat the skillet and add the solid shortening, using only enough to lay a film of oil on the surface of the pan. When the skillet is hot enough to scatter drops of water across the pan, start to cook the pancakes. Pour 2 tablespoons of batter into the pan and lift the pan, tilting it to position the batter all over the bottom of the pan. Let the pancake cook until bubbles form on the surface, and the bottom is browned. Turn the pancake to brown the other side. While second side is browning, spread a tablespoon of flaked ham on the pancake. When the pancake is browned, roll it up and serve to a hungry camper. Continue to cook the pancakes, one at a time, adding oil to the skillet as needed. Cook some of the pancakes without the ham, and serve the rollups with honey or jelly. This recipe will make 24–28 thin pancakes.

OATS AND FRUIT

One recipe of Bloated Oaties, Chapter 2, page 18
dry milk powder
water, either hot or cold

Use ½ cup oat mix per serving. Sprinkle 2 tablespoons dry milk powder over the oats and add ⅔ cup water. This cereal tastes good either hot or cold. If you are going to serve it hot, use boiling water and allow the cereal to sit for a few minutes before you eat it.

HOT DRINK & WARM BREAD

"When in doubt, boil water" is an adage many camp cooks take to heart. Certainly, hot water is a necessity for back-pack cooking. If you put a pot of water on to heat first thing in the morning, you and your fellow campers can enjoy a cup of hot coffee, cocoa or tea while you prepare the morning meal. If hitting the trail is a priority, place a foil-wrapped piece of one of the brought-from-home trail breads in your skillet and place the skillet over the pan of water on your stove. Even better is a sauce pan which fits into the larger pan of water and will absorb the heat from the pan of water like a double boiler. The bread will heat up as the coffee perks or the water boils. A glass of fruit drink, the warm bread with margarine and jelly and a cup of your favorite hot drink will get you started in a hurry.

▲▲▲▲▲▲▲▲▲▲▲▲▲▲▲▲▲▲▲▲▲▲▲▲▲▲▲▲▲▲▲▲

Soups & Chowders

Hot soup is a natural for lunch on layover days. The hearty chowders listed here are substantial enough to be served for dinner.

BOSTON STYLE CLAM CHOWDER

1 2.4-oz. package of Knorr Leek soup mix
2 single serving packets from a 2.5-oz. package
  Knorr Swiss potato soup
5 cups water
⅓ cup dry milk powder
1 6½-oz. can fancy mixed clams
Black pepper to taste

Put the dry milk powder and the soup mixes in a large pan. Stir to blend the flavors. Add the water and blend well. Cook the mixture over medium heat until it starts to boil, stirring constantly. Reduce the heat and cook for 8 minutes, stirring occasionally. Add the clams and the clam juice and continue to cook for 2 minutes, just long enough to heat the clams. Stir occasionally. Add black pepper to taste and serve with hearty rye crispbread slices. This recipe yields 5⅓ cups of hearty soup.

ASPARAGUS CHEESE SOUP

1 1.6-oz. package Knorr Asparagus soup mix
1 1.25-oz. package cheese sauce mix
4½ cups of water
1 6¾-oz. can of ham chunks (optional)
Dash of herb mix

Heat water to boiling and add the soup mix. Stir to blend and continue to cook over low heat, stirring constantly. Do not boil. Cook for 4 minutes, then add the cheese-sauce mix and the herb mix. Continue to cook for 2 minutes, stirring. Add the ham, if desired. Serve steaming hot with bannock or skillet bread. This recipe yields 5 cups or 4 generous servings.

ORIENTAL NOODLE SOUP WITH BEEF

2 3-oz. packages ramen noodle soup, oriental flavor
1 12-oz. can parboiled roast beef and gravy, steam roasted with gravy
2 tablespoons tomato paste
4 cups of water

Bring the water to a boil and add the noodles. Cook for 2 minutes, stirring. Add the can of beef with gravy and the tomato paste. Stir to blend and continue to cook for 2 more minutes. Remove the pan from the heat and add the 2 packets of seasoning from the soup packages. Serve the soup immediately, dividing the meat evenly into the soup mugs. This recipe will serve 4.

SPLIT PEA SOUP WITH HAM CHUNKS

1 2.4-oz. Knorr split pea with carrots soup mix
4 cups water
1 6¾-oz. ham chunks

Bring the water to a boil in a large pan. Stir the soup mix into the water and continue to cook until the soup comes to a boil, stirring constantly. Reduce the heat, cover the pan and continue to cook over low heat for 7 minutes, stirring occasionally. Add the ham chunks and any liquid in the can. Stir to blend the ingredients. Cook for an additional 2–3 minutes. Serve with skillet corn cakes or sesame crispbread. This recipe will make 4 generous servings.

MUSHROOM SOUP WITH CHICKEN

1 1.9-oz. Knorr mushroom soup mix
2 single-serving packets of Knorr potato soup
1 6¾-oz. can boned chicken with broth
5 cups cold water

Blend the dry soup mixes together in a large pan and add the cold water. Cook over a medium flame or fire, stirring, until the mixture comes to a boil. Continue to cook over a low flame for 5 minutes, stirring occasionally, then add the chicken and broth. Stir to blend the flavors and cook for another 2–3 minutes. This recipe yields 4 generous servings.

ITALIAN VEGETABLE SOUP WITH BEEF

1 2-oz. Knorr beefy vegetable soup mix
1 12-oz. can roast beef, with gravy
4 tablespoons tomato paste
½ cup crushed noodles
½ teaspoon herb mix
4 cups of cold water

Stir the tomato paste into the cold water in a large pan. Add the soup mix and stir to blend. Cook over a medium flame until the mixture starts to boil, stirring constantly. Add the herb mix and the crushed noodles. Cover and cook for 10 minutes. Add the beef and gravy and continue to cook, stirring occasionally, for 5 minutes. Adjust the seasonings and serve to 4 hungry campers.

QUICK CUPS OF SOUP FOR FAST STARTS

Instant soup mixes are available in a range of flavors to suit almost every taste. A quick cup will take the edge off the hunger as the main dinner course simmers on the fire. Split pea, potato and chicken are sure winners, and 2 tablespoons of tomato paste stirred into a cup of boiling water can be the basis for a tasty tomato soup. Just add seasoning salt and pepper; for more zest, add a pinch of herb mix. Any of these soups are ready in minutes. Don't think soup is only for lunch or dinner. A cup of hearty instant split pea soup with some real bacon bits sprinkled on top is a good way to start the day. Chicken soup is also a tasty breakfast addition. These soups are packaged in single-serving envelopes, four to a box. If you are camping in an area where fires are allowed, burn the boxes as they empty to reduce the weight and bulk of your pack.

TOMATO AND HERB FLAVORED MINESTRONE SOUP

1 2.8-oz. package Knorr homestyle minestrone soup
1 envelope herb flavored instant tomato soup
4½ cups water

Put the dry soup ingredients into a large saucepan and gradually add the water, stirring to blend with a wire whisk. Bring the mixture to a boil over medium high heat, stirring constantly. Reduce the heat and cover the pot. Continue to cook for 10 minutes, stirring occasionally. This recipe will make four 8-ounce servings.

MORE THAN CHICKEN NOODLE SOUP

1 2½-oz. package Knorr chicken flavor noodle
   soup mix
1 cup vermicelli
5½ cups water
1 chicken bouillion cube
1 5 or 6-oz. can chicken

Stir the contents of the soup package and
the vermicelli into the water in a large sauce
pan. Over high heat, stirring constantly, bring
the mixture to a boil. Add the bouillion cube
and stir until it dissolves. Lower the heat and
cover the pot. Continue to cook, stirring occasionally for 8 minutes. Add the chicken and
cook for another 2 minutes. This recipe will
make four 1½ cup servings.

LENTIL SOUP WITH PEPPERED SPAM

1 3.2-oz. package Knorr Homestyle harvest
   lentil soup mix
1 1-oz. package Knorr pepper sauce mix
1 12-oz. can Spam or other canned luncheon
   meat
5 cups water

Place the soup and pepper sauce mixes in a large pan and add the water, stirring with a wire whisk to blend. Bring the mixture to a boil over medium-high heat, stirring constantly. Cover the pot and lower the heat. Cook at a slow boil for 7 minutes.

While the soup is cooking remove the Spam from its can and cut into 1-inch cubes. Add the meat to the soup and cook an additional 3–5 minutes for a total of 10 to 12 minutes. This recipe will make 4 generous servings.

ORIENTAL NOODLE SOUP WITH SPAM

2 3-oz. packets of ramen pork-flavored oriental noodles
4 cups water
1 12-oz. can Spam or other canned luncheon meat
1 tablespoon margarine

In a large sauce pan bring 3 cups of the water to a boil and add the noodles from both packages. Cook the noodles for 3 minutes, then remove the pot from the stove and add the seasoning packet from ONE of the noodle packages.

Open the Spam and cut it into ¼-inch slices, then julienne the slices. In a skillet melt the margarine until it sizzles and then add the julienned meat. Sauté briefly, then add the remaining cup of water and the seasoning pouch from the second noodle packet. Simmer the meat in this sauce for a minute, then add the meat and sauce to the noodle soup in the large sauce pan. Reheat the soup, cooking for another minute or so. This will yield 4 cups of soup.

6

▲▲

One-Dish Meals

*T*he end of any day on the trail calls for a flavorful meal. The one-dish meals described below combine packaged freeze-dried foods and canned meats from supermarket shelves and provide nutrition as well as good taste. Repackaging some items before you leave home will ease the load. These recipes can be prepared for about half the cost of the freeze-dried, prepackaged dinners for four sold at specialty shops. Ingredients for a four-course dinner (soup, entree, drink and dessert) for four people made from these recipes will weigh about 10 ounces more than the specialty store package.

Tofu Protein Supplement

Tofu is the pale, buttery colored curd of soybeans. It has no distinctive flavor or aroma of its own, so it combines well with any of the main dish recipes and adds a good source of protein. It is inexpensive and keeps well on the trail.

The Mori Nu brand of tofu is hermetically sealed and will stay fresh for 10 months in a reasonably cool and dry environment without refrigeration, as long as it is unopened. It is sold in a 10.5-ounce package, just right for chopping into the noodle and rice dishes in these recipes.

BEEF, STROGANOFF STYLE

An ideal first-night-on-the-trail dinner, offering flavor and nutrition. The tofu is an option, but is suggested for added protein and fat.

1 12-oz. can Roast Beef, with gravy
1 .87-oz. package mushroom gravy mix
1 4.3-oz. package freeze-dried Stroganoff
  noodles
1 10.5-oz. package Mori Nu tofu, optional
4 cups water
½ teaspoon butter buds, optional
1 cup ½-inch noodles

Pour the mushroom gravy powder into a large pot and add 1 cup of cold water. Stir until the powder is absorbed into the water. Add 3 additional cups of water and stir to blend. Bring the gravy and water mixture to a boil then add the contents of the stroganoff noodle package, the butter buds, and the noodles to the boiling water. Cook, stirring occasionally, for 5 minutes. Cut the tofu into 1-inch cubes and add it to the noodles and gravy. Add the can of roast beef and gravy, stirring to distribute the meat through the noodle mixture. Remove the pan from the stove. The mixture will thicken as it sits. This will serve 4 hungry campers.

CHICKEN WITH POTATOES AND MUSHROOM GRAVY

2 6¾ cans boned chicken in broth
2 3.5-oz. foil packages of freeze-dried chicken and mushroom flavored potatoes
1 .87-oz. package chicken gravy mix
5 cans water
A dash of Herb Mix (see page 24), optional

Put the chicken gravy powder into a large pot and gradually stir in 1 cup of water and the herb mix. Add the remaining 4 cups of water and stir to blend. Bring the contents to a boil then add the packages of potatoes. Cook, stirring occasionally, for 6 minutes. Add the chicken to the pot and stir well to distribute. Continue cooking for 4 or 5 minutes or until the potatoes are tender. This recipe is enough for 4 generous servings.

SPANISH-STYLE RICE WITH BEEF

    1 12-oz. can beef with gravy
    1 4.5-oz. foil package of Spanish rice
    4 tablespoons tomato paste
    3 cups water
    1 cup instant rice
    salt and pepper to taste

Bring the water to a boil in a large pan. Add the tomato paste and stir to blend. Stir in the Spanish rice and cook for 7 minutes. Add the canned beef and stir. Continue to cook for 3 minutes, then add the instant rice. Remove the pot from the stove and let the mixture thicken for 5 minutes. Adjust the seasonings and serve to 4 campers.

SCALLOPED POTATOES WITH HAM AND CHEESE SAUCE

A foil-wrapped package of scalloped potatoes will combine with a can of chunked ham and an envelope of cheese sauce mix for a tasty meal.

2 3.8-oz. foil packages of freeze-dried scalloped potatoes
1 6¾-oz. can chunked ham
1 1.25-oz. package cheese sauce mix
5 cups of water
⅓ cup dry milk powder

Put the cheese sauce mix and the dry milk powder in a large pot and gradually add 1 cup of water. Add the 4 remaining cups of water and bring to a boil. Add the packages of potatoes, and cook for 7 or 8 minutes before adding the ham. Continue to cook for 3 minutes. Remove the pan from the stove and let the mixture thicken before serving. This recipe will make 4 servings.

CHICKEN & CHICKEN-FLAVORED NOODLES

A quick one-pot meal, good for dinner or lunch on a layover day.

2 6¾-oz. cans of boned chicken with broth
1 4.5-oz. foil-wrapped package of butter
   flavored noodles and sauce
1 cup dry noodles
2 single-serving envelopes of cream of chicken
   instant soup
5 cups water
½-teaspoon butter buds, optional

Bring the water to a boil. Add the soup powder and the butter buds. Stir briskly. Stir in the contents of the noodle package and the dry noodles and continue to boil, stirring occasionally, for 5 minutes. Add the chicken and broth and continue to cook for another 4 minutes. This recipe serves 4 and allows for 3 ounces of chicken per serving.

NOTE: Tofu can be added to this one dish recipe for additional nutrition.

TUNA FLAVORED NOODLES WITH MUSHROOM SAUCE

2 2½-oz. foil packages butter-flavored noodles
4 cups water
2 teaspoons butter crystals
1 6½-oz. can tuna, drained (can be either water pack or oil pack)
SAUCE:
1 .9-oz. Knorr mushroom sauce mix
1¼ cups water
⅔ cup dry milk powder

Bring 4 cups of water to a boil with the butter crystals in a large pan over medium-high heat. Stir in the packages of noodles. Cook for 7–8 minutes or until noodles are done. Remove the pot from the fire and cover. In a small saucepan, combine the milk powder and the mushroom sauce mix. Stir in the 1¼ cup of water and blend well. Stirring constantly with a wire whisk, cook over medium heat until the mixture comes to a boil. Reduce the heat and cook the sauce for 2 minutes or until the sauce thickens. Add the can of drained tuna, separating the fish into small pieces. Cook just until heated, then add this mixture to the buttered noodles, stirring gently to coat the noodles with the sauce. This recipe makes 4 heaping cups.

SALMON WITH RICE AND BROCCOLI

1 6½ to 7½-oz. can salmon
1 4.7-oz. foil package of freeze-dried rice with
   broccoli with cheddar sauce
1 cup instant rice
salt and pepper to taste
pinch of herb mix
3 cups water

Bring the water to a boil. Add the foil package of rice and broccoli and the herb mix and cook for 10 minutes. Add the instant rice and stir well. Drain the liquid from the can of salmon and add the fish to the rice mixture. Cover and remove from the stove. Let the mixture sit for 5 minutes. Taste before adding salt and pepper. NOTE: Any fish you catch can be added to this recipe. Clean your catch, cut it into bite-size bits and cook with the rice and broccoli, before adding the canned salmon and instant rice.

SALMON AND SEASONED POTATOES

1 6½ to 7½-oz. can salmon
2 3.8-oz. packages potatoes with sour cream
  and chive flavors
dash of herb mix
4 cups water

Bring the water to a boil and add the herb mix and the potatoes. Cook, stirring occasionally for 8 minutes. Drain the salmon and add it to the potato mixture. Cook an additional 3–4 minutes. Let stand for a few minutes before serving. The mixture will thicken as it stands. This recipe will serve 4.

SWEET & SOUR SPAM WITH BUTTERED NOODLES

2 2½-oz. foil packages butter-flavored noodles
4 cups water
2 teaspoons dry butter crystals
1 12-oz. can Spam or other canned luncheon
    meat
1 tablespoon margarine
SAUCE:
1 cup water
4 tablespoons freeze-dried pineapple chunks
4 tablespoons tomato paste
2 teaspoons sugar
4 tablespoons sweet pickle relish (or 5
    individual packets of relish)

Bring the 4 cups of water to a boil. Add the dry butter crystals and the noodles from both packages. Cook the noodles for 7–8 minutes or until done. Remove from the stove and set aside.

Slice the Spam into 8 equal slices. Melt half of the margarine in a skillet and add as many slices of the Spam slices as your skillet will hold. Brown the meat slices on both sides, adding margarine as needed, then remove them from the pan. Continue this process until all the slices are browned. Set them aside, covered with a pot lid or piece of foil.

Pour a single cup of water into the hot skillet and add the chunks of pineapple. Add the sugar and boil for a minute or so until the pineapple begins to soften. Add the tomato paste, stirring well to blend. Stir in the pickle relish. Add the cooked Spam slices to the sweet and sour sauce. Serve the meat over the noodles. This recipe will make four 1-cup servings of noodles and allows for 2 slices for each of 4 campers.

CREAMED SALMON & PEAS WITH POTATOES

2 3.8-oz. packages scalloped potatoes
4 cups water
⅔ cup dry milk powder
2 teaspoons butter crystals
1 7½-oz. can red sockeye salmon
1 1-oz. package freeze-dried instant peas

Place the dry milk powder in a large pan and gradually add the water. Stir in the butter crystals. Add the contents of both packages of potatoes and the peas to the water and bring the mixture to a boil over high heat, stirring occasionally. Cook the potato mixture over medium heat at a slow boil for 10 minutes.

While the potatoes cook, open the can of salmon and extract all the white ring-like pieces of cartilage and any dark fish skin from the salmon meat. When the potatoes are done, add the salmon, gently stirring to mingle the flavors. This will yield four 1¼-cup servings. If you are fortunate enough to be camping in salmon country, you can substitute fresh salmon in this recipe. Merely add salmon pieces and a cup of water to the large pot before you begin to cook the potatoes and peas. Cook the salmon pieces for 2–3 minutes, then remove them and proceed with the recipe, adding the fish at the end of the recipe as directed.

CORNED BEEF & CHEESE POTATOES

⅔ cup dry milk powder
4 cups water
1 12-oz. can corned beef
2 4.3-oz. packages potatoes au gratin
Approximately 4 tablespoons cheddar cheese from a 4⅝-oz. pressurized can of pasteurized processed cheese

Put the milk powder in a large pan and gradually add water as you stir the mixture.

Stir in the potato package contents and bring the mixture to a boil. Continue to cook for 10 minutes or until the potatoes are softened. Stir in the cheese directly from the container, estimating the amount. This cheese will come out of the can as you press the nozzle. Stir the cheese into the potatoes to combine the flavors. Open the corned beef and add the meat to the potato-cheese mixture, flaking the corned beef as it is added. This will serve 4 campers.

HAM WITH TOMATO & HERB FLAVORED PASTA

1 envelope herb-flavored instant tomato soup
4 cups water
2 tablespoons tomato paste
1 4½-oz. package tomato and herb flavored
  pasta
1 cup vermicelli
1 6¾-oz. can ham

Bring the water to a boil over high heat and stir in the tomato paste and the instant soup. Stir in the package of flavored noodles and the vermicelli and simmer for 10–11 minutes. Add the ham and cook until heated through. This recipe will serve 4.

CHICKEN & RICE

1 4.6-oz. package rice and sauce
1 teaspoon butter crystals
3 cups water
1 5- to 6-oz. can chicken, either white or dark
   meat
1 cup instant cooking rice
SAUCE:
1 .87-oz. envelope chicken gravy
1 cup water

Place the contents of the rice and sauce package into a large pan with the butter crystals and 3 cups of water. Bring to a boil and cook for 10–12 minutes. Add the instant cooking rice, cover the pot and remove it from the heat source.

In a small saucepan or skillet, put the chicken gravy mix. Add the 1 cup of water and blend. Cook the gravy over medium high heat, stirring until it boils. Continue to cook for 2–3 minutes, then add the chicken. Blend well. Serve the rice on plates or in bowls and pour the chicken and gravy over the rice portions. Makes 4 large servings.

TUNA-FLAVORED RICE & PASTA

1 can tuna, drained (either water or oil pack)
1 4.8-oz. box of rice and pasta mix with
  cauliflower and cheese
4 teaspoons of butter crystals
1 1¼-oz. packet of cheese sauce mix
1½ cups instant cooking rice
5 cups water

Place the cheese sauce mix in a large sauce pan with the rice and pasta mix and the butter crystals.

Gradually add the water, blending with a wire whisk. Bring the mixture to a boil, then lower the heat. Simmer this mixture for 10 minutes, then add the instant cooking rice. Cover the pan and remove it from the heat. Let it stand 5 minutes or until the instant rice is tender. Mix well and add the tuna fish. Return the pot to the stove and cook just until tuna is heated through. This recipe will make 4 generous servings.

TUNA AND PASTA IN GARLIC SAUCE

1 6½-oz. can tuna, drained (either oil or water pack)
1 4¾-oz. package of pasta shells in garlic sauce
1 cup vermicelli
¼ cup of powder from a 1.8-oz. packet of Knorr white sauce mix
1 1-oz. package of instant freeze-dried peas
⅔ cup dry milk powder
1 chicken bouillion cube
4 cups water

Place the white sauce mix and the dry milk powder in a large saucepan and add 1 cup of water, stirring to blend with a wire whisk. When the mixture is smooth gradually add the remainder of the water, the pasta shells in garlic sauce and the vermicelli.

Bring this mixture to a boil and add the bouillion cube and the dried peas. Cook for 10 minutes, stirring occasionally. Add the tuna fish and cook for another minute or two, to heat the fish. This recipe will make 4 generous servings.

CORNED BEEF AND POTATO PIE

1 12-oz. can corned beef
2 2-oz. packages Borden's country store
  mashed potatoes
⅔ cup dry milk powder
2 teaspoons butter crystals
3 cups water
Seasoning salt and pepper as needed

Place the dry milk powder and the butter
crystals in a large sauce pan and add 1 cup of
water. Stir with a wire whisk until smooth
then add the remainder of the water. Bring
this mixture to a boil. Remove the pan from
the heat and immediately add the potato
flakes from both packages. Stir well to
moisten all the potato flakes. Set the potatoes
aside.

Open the can of corned beef and place the
meat in a large skillet, pressing the meat into
a flat, even layer. Cook over medium heat until the meat is slightly brown and crisp. Spoon
the mashed potatoes on top and spread them
into an even layer. Add seasoning salt and
pepper as desired. Cut the pie into slices and
serve. This recipe will make 4 large servings
or 6 medium-size pieces of meat pie.

TRAIL STEW

1 envelope herb-flavored instant tomato soup
1 1-oz. package of instant freeze dried peas
5 cups water
1 12-oz. can roast beef
1 3.4-oz. packages beef and mushroom
    potatoes
1 cup ½-inch noodles
1 envelope beef-flavored onion soup mix
2 tablespoons tomato paste

Combine the onion and tomato soup powders in a large saucepan. Gradually add water to blend the ingredients to a smooth paste. Add the remainder of the water, stirring to blend. Stir in the tomato paste.

Add the entire contents of the beef and mushroom flavored noodles, the cup of ½-inch noodles and the peas to the saucepan. Stir well to blend the ingredients. Bring the food to a boil, stirring occasionally. Cook for 10 minutes, then add the can of roast beef with any gravy in the can. Add more water now if you prefer a juicy stew. Cook until the meat is heated through, about 2–3 minutes. Serve in large mugs or cups to 4 campers.

TRAIL LAPSKAUS

(Lapskaus is from a Norwegian immigrant recipe popular in the U.S. during the Great Depression of the 1930's. Potatoes were cheap and could be added to stretch the recipe to feed as many mouths as necessary.)

> **1 12-oz. can corned beef**
> **1 3.8-oz. package scalloped potatoes**
> **1 tablespoon dehydrated onion**
>   **flakes**
> **2 cups water**
> **1 teaspoon butter crystals**

Bring the water to a boil, add the butter crystals and the package of potatoes. Cook for 7–8 minutes, then add onion flakes and partially mash the potatoes with a cooking spoon. Cook for 3 minutes or until the potatoes are soft. Add the corned beef to the pan. Heat the meat through, then spoon the mixture onto pieces of Wasa hearty rye bread.

This is an easy meal with little cleanup required. The open-faced sandwiches can be eaten with fingers and no plates are necessary.

SPAM WITH NOODLES & CHEESE

2 4¾-oz. packages noodles and cheese sauce
3¼ cups water
4 teaspoons butter crystals
1 12-oz. can Spam, or other pre-cooked canned
  luncheon meat
1 tablespoon margarine
1 individual plastic packet of mustard
¼ cup water

Bring the 3 cups of water to a boil and add
both packages of the noodles and cheese and
the butter crystals. Cook for 10 minutes.
While the noodles cook, open the can of Spam
and place the meat on a clean surface. Cut the
meat into 1-inch cubes. Heat the margarine in
a skillet until it sizzles and add the meat
cubes. Brown the meat on all sides, then add
the mustard and ¼ cup of water, stirring to
blend. Cook, making sure the cubes of meat
are coated with the mustard sauce. Add the
meat to the noodles and cheese mixture and
stir to blend. Serve to 4 campers.

▲▲

7

Desserts

*F*reeze-dried desserts can be found in mountaineering stores or campers' supply catalogs. Varieties of freeze-dried fruit cobblers and ice creams to be reconstituted at the campsite taste very good. Unfortunately, they are very expensive.

One cheaper, light-weight dessert is pressed fruit rolls. They satisfy a sweet tooth and add vitamin C to your diet. But for economy and good taste, instant puddings are a backpacker's best bet. Instant pudding on the supermarket shelf is packaged in a paper pouch inside a cardboard box. The pouch should be removed from the box and sealed in a plastic bag for safe, waterproof packing.

TANGY TAPIOCA

⅓ cup instant tapioca
2½ cups water
⅔ cup Tang
dash of salt
⅓ cup sugar

Put the instant tapioca in a saucepan with the sugar and salt. Combine the Tang and the water and stir to blend. Add the Tang to the saucepan and stir well. Set aside and allow the mixture to steep for 10 minutes. Place the saucepan over a medium fire, and stirring occasionally bring the mixture to a boil. Remove the pudding from the fire and allow to sit for 20–30 minutes. This fruity dessert can be eaten warm or cold. It is particularly good served warm over a piece of Best Guides Bread, (see Chap. 2).

CHEESECAKE

1 box Jello-brand Real Cheesecake, 11-oz. size
   (includes graham cracker crumbs for crust)
3 tablespoons sugar
⅓ cup margarine

1½ cups cool water
⅔ cup dry milk powder
2 8-inch aluminum pie pans, OR
1 8-inch aluminum pie pan and a piece of
   aluminum foil, 9″ square

Remove the two pouches of ingredients from
the box before you leave home. Pack the
pouches in an air tight plastic bag.

To prepare the pie crust, place the margarine in the pie pan over a medium flame.
When the margarine is melted remove the
pan from the stove. Add the contents of the
graham crumbs package and the sugar to the
margarine, blending well with your fingers.
When the crumbs are coated with the margarine, firmly press the mixture into the pan
using your cooking spoon. Set the crust aside
while you mix the filling.

Mix the dry milk powder with the water. Stir until well blended than beat with a wire whisk in slow even strokes for about 3 minutes. When the mixture is smooth and beginning to thicken, pour it into the cooled graham crust. Cover the pie with a second aluminum pan or a piece of foil and set it aside to cool. OPTION: If you are in an area in which wild strawberries or blueberries grow, you can make a compote to put on top of your cheesecake.

VANILLA PUDDING

1 3½-oz. package instant vanilla
   pudding
2 cups of cool water
⅔ cup dry milk powder
4 tablespoons of crumbled almond toffee

Pour the contents of the pudding pouch into a small saucepan (or plastic bowl, if you carry one). Add the milk powder and blend. Stir in the cool water and beat with a wire whisk until the mixture is smooth and beginning to thicken. Divide the pudding into four equal portions and let stand 5 minutes. Top with crumbled almond toffee and serve.

CHOCOLATE COCONUT PUDDING

1 3½-oz. package instant chocolate
  pudding
2 cups cool water
⅔ cup dry milk powder
4 tablespoons coconut

Combine the pudding mix and dry milk powder. Add the water and blend well. Beat with wire whisk until mixture begins to thicken. Add the coconut, divide into 4 equal portions and let stand 5 minutes before serving.

BLUEBERRY COMPOTE

1 to 2 cups berries
3 to 4 tablespoons of sugar/cinammon mixture
  (Chapter 2,)
1 tablespoon instant tapioca
¼- to ½-cup water

Put the tapioca, the sugar/cinnamon mixture and the water in a small saucepan. Let the mixture stand for 5 minutes, then add the blueberries and cook over a medium flame until the mixture begins to boil. Remove the pan from the stove and allow the compote to cool thoroughly. When the fruit is cool, spread it on top of the cheesecake. This mixture can be used for a topping for vanilla pudding as well.

PISTACHIO PUDDING

1 3½-oz. package instant pistachio pudding
2 cups cool water
⅔ cup dry milk powder
4 tablespoons trail mix, nuts or coconut,
    optional

Combine the pudding mix and the dry milk powder and add the water. Blend well with a wire whisk, pour 4-oz. servings into 4 bowls and let stand for 5 minutes. Top with trail mix, nuts or coconut and serve.

ROLLS OF READY-MIXED PUDDING SURPRISES

Chocolate and butterscotch pudding rolls can be found on your grocer's shelves, usually near the dried cereals. These rolls are similar to the fruit rollups discussed earlier. They are quite good eaten straight from the pack (don't forget to remove the clear plastic wrapping.) To make them even tastier try unrolling them, filling them with coconut, peanut-butter chips or crumbled almond toffee chips, and re-rolling them. Tuck the sides in before re-rolling to assure the surprise contents don't spill out.

▲▲▲

8

The Fisherman's Catch

A fishing license can be a meal ticket as well as a passport to outdoor fun. Fresh fish are good to eat anytime, but they are a special treat for a backpacking party.

Fish are easier to cook than they are to catch and clean, so the smart cook will quickly volunteer to do all the cooking if the rest of the party does the cleaning.

Most backpackers will want to prepare their catch for pan frying. Small fish can be fried whole, while larger ones should be filleted or cut into steaks that will fit the pan.

To clean a pan-sized fish, grasp it by the tail and remove the scales by scraping toward the head with a dull knife, fish scaler or the edge of a large spoon. Make cuts on either side of the fins and pull them out with pliers. Get all the bones. Make a V-shaped cut just behind the vent. Cut deeply behind the head and

along the sides of the belly to join up with the cut at the vent. Don't puncture the stomach or intestines of the fish. The head, viscera and the skin of the belly will come away together. Wash out any clotted blood along the backbone, and the fish is ready for cooking.

Larger fish may be filleted with a sharp knife with a thin, flexible blade. Hold the fish by the head and make a cut just behind the head to the backbone, taking care not to cut through the backbone or cut into the abdominal cavity. Slice along the backbone down to the ribs on either side of the dorsal fins. Peel the flesh back and extend the cut deeper to the end of the ribs. Make a shallow cut along the side of the fish to remove the fillet from the ribs.

To remove skin from the fillets, place the fillet, skin down, on a flat surface. Start from the tail and work the knife blade between the skin and the flesh. Hold the skin and, keeping the knife flat, gradually work the thin blade between the skin and the fillet up to the head. When you are finished, you will have a boneless fillet ready for the pan.

Other large fish can be scaled and cleaned using a technique like that suggested for pan fish. Steaks about 1-inch thick can be cut crosswise from the body of the large fish. The skin is usually left on these steaks.

Catfish must be cleaned in a different way. Remove the fins and cut through the skin all the way around the fish just behind the head. With a pair of pliers, pull the skin toward the tail. When the skin is peeled off, cut through the backbone just behind the head and pull the head away. The viscera will come with the head.

Clean out the body cavity to complete the job. Fry small catfish whole. Larger fish can be cut into steaks. All catfish have sharp spines on either side of the head and in the dorsal fin. The spines can make convenient handles when you are cleaning the fish, but they can also inflict painful wounds if you are careless.

Opinions vary regarding disposal of fish-heads and viscera. Some campers leave remains on the shore for turtles and birds while others bury the trash in the woods. Whichever course you follow, be sure to keep these leftovers far away from your campsite to avoid attracting bears and other animals.

Pan Frying

All you need to pan fry fish is a skillet, oil, seasonings, flour or cornmeal and a pan-sized piece of fish.

Shake the damp fish pieces in a plastic bag of cornmeal or flour mixed with seasoning salt.

Sprinkle a small pinch of herb mix (pg 00) on the fish.

Heat about ⅛-inch of oil in a skillet. When the oil is simmering, put in the fish pieces.

Cook the fish until it is still moist but flakes easily with a fork. (Whole pan fish 6 to 8 inches long or 1-inch steaks will require about 5 minutes per side. Thinner fillets will cook more quickly.)

FRESH FISH CHOWDER

To stretch a limited catch to serve 4, make a chowder.

¾ to 1 pound of fish
1 3.8-oz. package of freeze-dried scalloped
　potatoes
2 tablespoons margarine
2 teaspoons onion flakes
⅔ cup dry milk powder
3½ cups water
Herb seasonings to taste

Mix the water and dry milk powder in the largest cooking pot. Cut the fish into 1-inch pieces. Bring the milk and the margarine to the boiling point and add the scalloped potatoes. Boil over medium heat for 8 minutes or until the potatoes are tender. Add the fish, onion flakes and approximately ¼ teaspoon of herb seasonings. Cover the pan and simmer for 12 minutes or until the fish flakes easily. Adjust the seasoning to taste during the last 2 or 3 minutes of cooking.

▲▲

9

Base Camp Meals

*B*etween home and trail, backpackers often set up a base camp. This campsite near the trail head may be used for only a single night or might be inhabited off and on for a week or more.

No matter how base camp is used, cooking is easier there. In base camp it may be possible to use charcoal and even wood fires in addition to small stoves. A folding grill and a Dutch oven, items unsuitable or too heavy for backpacking, can be stored at base camp. Just these two utensils and some hot coals can make it possible to add a wide range of recipes to the menu. If a camp table or fireplace is also available, the luxury may be overwhelming.

Eggs, fresh fruits, fresh meat, yeast breads and some dairy products that wouldn't fare well in a backpack can be part of a base camp menu. All the recipes included below assume the availability of charcoal for cooking. All recipes, as they do elsewhere in this book, serve four.

Charcoal Fires

(If you know how to cook with charcoal, skip this section.) Pressed charcoal briquets burn evenly and last longer than irregular charcoal pieces. To start a briquet fire quickly, make a chimney from a two-pound coffee can. Cut the ends out of the can and punch holes up and down the length of the cylinder. Fill the chimney with briquets and crumpled paper. Light the paper to start the fire. When the briquets turn gray, remove the chimney and spread the coals evenly. Charcoal lighter or kerosene will speed up the process. Move the lighter fluid container away from area before lighting the charcoal. *Never use gasoline to light charcoal.*

Test the heat of your fire by holding your hand six to eight inches above the coals. Count slowly. A really hot fire will make your hand uncomfortable after a single count. A slow fire will feel too hot after a count of four.

Garlic bread served with spaghetti makes a base camp meal that is quick, easy and very filling. It is an especially good choice for arrival night at base camp, because the sauce has been cooked in your kitchen at home and needs only to be heated.

GARLIC BREAD

Bring along Italian bread from your favorite bakery. Wrapped in foil and plastic, bread will stay fresh for two or three days. It is delicious with any dinner and also makes good French toast for breakfast.

To spice up the bread for a spaghetti dinner, take along a tablespoon of garlic powder in a plastic bag. Slice a couple of loaves of bread and spread the pieces with margarine. Sprinkle each piece with a little garlic powder, rewrap the loaves in foil. Place the loaves on the grill over a hot charcoal fire. Turn the bread every four or five minutes. Check it after 10 minutes. It's done when the crust is crispy and the margarine melted and warm.

SPAGHETTI SAUCE

1 medium-sized onion, diced
½ large green pepper, diced
1 large celery rib, diced
1 garlic clove, minced (or equivalent garlic
    powder)

2 tablespoons cooking oil
1½ pounds beef (chuck or round steak),
   ground
½ tablespoon salt
¼ teaspoon black pepper
½ tablespoon dried oregano
½ tablespoon ground cumin seed
1 tablespoon flour
1 can (28 ounces) tomatoes
1 can (six ounces) tomato paste
1 tablespoon sugar

Saute the vegetables in the cooking oil in a
large saucepan. Add the beef and brown it
quickly. Stir to mix the vegetables and meat,
then add the salt, pepper, oregano, cumin seed
and flour. Stir to blend. Reduce the heat and
immediately add the tomatoes. Using a large
knife and fork, cut the tomatoes into very

small pieces as they cook. Add the tomato paste and stir it well. Blend in the sugar, reduce the heat and let the sauce simmer for 45 minutes to an hour, stirring the sauce occasionally to prevent scorching. Remove the sauce from the heat to cool. Place the cooled sauce in a 2-quart plastic container. (Rinse it with very cold water first, and the container will not be stained.)

Cover the container tightly and freeze it. Pack it in a travel cooler for the trip to base camp. Remove it from the cooler as soon as you reach your camp. Place the sauce in a pot and simmer it over a slow fire.

Bring a large pot of water and 2 teaspoons of salt to a boil and add 1½ pounds of uncooked spaghetti. Boil the spaghetti, uncovered, for 10 to 12 minutes. Remove it from the fire when it is done.

Drain off the water. (A plastic collander is very useful here.) Rinse the spaghetti with 2 cups of cold water to remove excess starch.

Serve on plates, pour about a cup of sauce over each serving and add grated parmesan cheese.

Leftover sauce will keep about 2 days in a camp cooler.

SPARERIBS WITH STORD'S BARBECUE SAUCE

(Prepare this dish at home, freeze it, and put it on the grill at base camp.)

Pork spareribs, about 1 lb. per person, cut into
    10 rib sections
Stord's Barbecue Sauce:
1 cup tomato catsup
¼ cup lemon juice
2 tablespoons brown sugar
1 tablespoon soy sauce
1 tablespoon horseradish or dijon-style
    mustard
1 tablespoon grated fresh onion *or* 1 teaspoon
    dehydrated onion flakes
½ teaspoon salt
½ teaspoon black pepper
¼ teaspoon dried oregano
¼ teaspoon Tabasco sauce
¼ teaspoon cayenne pepper

Combine all the sauce ingredients in a small saucepan and simmer them for 10 minutes. Remove the pan from the heat and cool. While the sauce cools, parboil the spareribs for 15–20 minutes. Remove the ribs from the water and allow them to cool. Stir the cooled sauce to blend the flavors and pour it over the spareribs. Place the sauced ribs, along with all the sauce, into large zippered freezer bags.

When you get to base camp, build a charcoal fire and when the briquets turn grey, grill the spareribs for 15–20 minutes, turning at intervals and basting with the sauce from the freezer bag.

DUTCH OVEN POT ROAST

1 2-pound boneless chuck roast
1 tablespoon vegetable shortening or suet
   trimmed from the roast
1 large onion, sliced
1 teaspoon herb mix
4 carrots, cleaned and cut into 3-inch pieces
4 white potatoes, peeled and quartered *or* 8–10
   small red-skinned potatoes, scrubbed
Seasoning salt
Pepper

Start a charcoal fire with your coffee can chimney (pg. 81). Add briquets to the fire until you have 40 or 50 going. When the briquets begin to get grey around the edges, put 18–20 of them to one side. Level the remaining coals and set the oven pot on them to pre-heat.

Add vegetable shortening or suet to the pot. When the fat is hot, brown the chuck well on one side. Turn the meat over and sprinkle it with seasoning salt, pepper, herb mix and sliced onion. Place the lid on the Dutch oven and shovel the briquets previously set aside onto the top of the flat lid. Let the meat cook for an hour or so, adding more briquets to the fire as needed. Using pot holders or cloths, remove the lid and add the cleaned and cut vegetables. Let the vegetables cook for 25–30 minutes, or until they are done.

CINNAMON APPLE CHOPS

½ cup apple jelly
¼ cup melted butter or
   margarine
3 tablespoons lemon juice
1 teaspoon prepared mustard
½ teaspoon ground cinnamon
4 early cooking apples
8 pork chops

Prepare 4 pieces of aluminum foil, each 10 × 18 inches. Put the first 5 ingredients for the basting sauce in a small saucepan or skillet; heat and stir. Peel and slice the apples. Lightly butter the center of the foil pieces. Lay the slices from one apple on each piece of foil. Drizzle some of the apple-cinnamon sauce over the apples, 1 teaspoon for each apple. Securely seal the foil pouches.

Set the grill 4 inches above the hot coals and place the pork chops on the grill. Baste them thoroughly with apple-cinnamon basting sauce. Broil the pork chops for 35 minutes, turning and basting them frequently. During the last 25 minutes of cooking time, lay the foil-wrapped packages of apples on the grill. Avoid puncturing the foil with your meat fork as you turn the pork chops. After 25 minutes, remove the apple packets from the grill; open the packages and test the apples with a meat fork. The apples should be soft to the touch. Reseal the packets and place them at the edge of the grill to keep them warm.

STEAK DINNER

Club, T-bones, or porterhouse steaks are delicious prepared on a grill over charcoal. A thickness of ¾-to-1 inch is about right for any of these steaks. Allow one steak for each hiker. A little seasoning salt and pepper are all that is needed. Freeze the raw steaks at home in individual plastic bags.

Baked Potatoes can be scrubbed well at home and wrapped in foil. At base camp, unwrap the potatoes and place them in a large pot of water to parboil. Cover them and let them boil for 20–25 minutes. Take them out of the water and re-wrap them in the foil. Place the wrapped potatoes in a bed of charcoal and let them cook for 20–30 minutes. Cook the steaks on a grill over the bed of charcoal. Because you washed the potatoes at home, the hot water will be clean enough to be used for doing the dishes after dinner.

Put the steaks on the grill 3 inches from the heat. Let the steaks smoke for 30 seconds, then turn them. Let the steaks sizzle for another 30 seconds on the second side. Many modern-day cooks insist a steak should be turned only once. However, when a steak 1 inch thick or less is cooked on one side for a period of time, the natural juices rise to the uncooked side and in turning the meat these juices are lost in the fire. By searing the meat on both sides before the real cooking starts you save some of the juices.

Broiling times for steaks of this thickness:
Rare: 5 to 8 minutes per side
Medium rare: 8 to 10 minutes per side
Well done: 12 to 15 minutes per side

Vegetables

In the summertime, when backpacking activity is at a peak, so are local garden crops. Roadside fruit and vegetable stands can be a good source of fresh-picked produce for base camp.

CORN ON THE COB IN A KETTLE

A large kettle of water, boiled for 10 minutes
2 cups fresh whole milk
1 tablespoon white sugar
Sweet white corn, husked and cleaned, 1–2
  ears per person

Bring the water to a boil, and add the milk and sugar. When the liquid starts to boil, reduce the heat and add the ears of corn. When the liquid returns to a near boil, cover the kettle and remove it from the heat. The corn will cook in the hot water for 8–10 minutes. Remove the corn from the water, serve with margarine, salt and pepper.

STEAMED CORN IN FOIL

Yellow corn can be prepared in the coals while the steaks, chops or ribs grill. Pull the green outer husks from as many ears of corn as you have hikers. Do not remove these husks, rather "peel" the ear of corn as you would a banana. Carefully remove the yellow corn silk from the kernels of corn on the cob. Re-wrap the corn husks around the ears of corn, sprinkle them liberally with clean water and wrap each ear in a piece of aluminum foil.

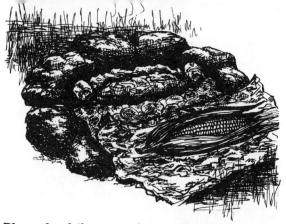

Place the foil wrapped corn directly into the hot coals and cook for 15–20 minutes. Serve with margarine, salt and pepper. A plate of raw vegetables—slices of cucumbers, zucchini and tomatoes along with a few small scallions—will top off this Steak Dinner.

Serve fresh fruit for dessert or wait until later and share a pot of chocolate fondue (see recipe, page 98).

Breakfast

BREAKFAST IN A SKILLET

3 leftover cold boiled potatoes
5 tablespoons of margarine
1 cup of ham pieces
salt and pepper
4 fresh eggs

Slice the potatoes; there should be about 2 cups of slices. Melt the margarine in the largest skillet you have. Brown the potato slices and ham pieces, stirring them until the food is warmed through. Sprinkle the potatoes with salt and pepper. In a small bowl or pot beat the eggs with a whisk until they are smooth and yellow. Add the eggs to the ingredients in the skillet and stir until the eggs are set. Serve hot.

PANCAKES AND HAM

Pancake mixes from the supermarket are easy to prepare and very good. To some you add milk and fresh eggs while others require only the addition of water. With the first type, whole milk or a combination of evaporated milk and water work equally well. Also add a tablespoon of extra oil. For non-fat dry milk mixes, use 2 tablespoons of melted margarine.

To cook, heat a well-oiled griddle or skillet until a water drop in the pan forms round beads and skitters across the surface. With a cup, pour about ¼ cup of batter into the pan for each pancake. Cook the pancakes until many bubbles start to form on the uncooked side. Turn them and cook the other side. Turn the cakes only once. Serve them with margarine, honey, syrup, jam or jelly.

Canned ham fries up easily in ¼-inch thick pieces. (Remove the gelatin around the ham.) Place the slices in a skillet in which you have melted a tablespoon of margarine. The canned ham is already cooked, so it is only necessary to fry it long enough to heat it through and brown it to taste. Some people prefer ham tender and pink while others like it with the edges frizzled and browned. Either way it goes well with pancakes, French toast or eggs.

FRENCH TOAST

3 eggs
1 cup of milk (whole, evaporated or dry milk powder)
½ cup pancake mix
1 tablespoon sugar
3 tablespoons margarine, or more as needed
Italian bread, 2 to 3 slices per person

In a small pan, mix the eggs and milk with a French whisk. Add the pancake mix and sugar and blend well. In a small skillet melt the margarine. Cut Italian bread into ½-inch slices and dip them into the batter. Place the egg-covered slices in the skillet and cook over low heat until they are lightly brown. Brown both sides. Serve the toast with syrup, honey or jelly.

CANNED BACON

Canned bacon is often cheaper than packaged bacon and requires no refrigeration if unopened. Canned bacon slices are usually thicker than the commonly sold packaged meat and require a bit more cooking time. The slices are wrapped in a paper liner and sealed in a vacuum tin. Be careful to remove the paper before placing the bacon in the pan. Start with a cold skillet with no grease or oil. Cook the slices over medium heat and pour off the rendered bacon fat as necessary to insure proper browning. A pound of canned bacon and four eggs make a good breakfast for four hikers. Any uncooked bacon must be refrigerated.

Desserts

DUTCH OVEN PEACH COBBLER

A two-quart Dutch oven is an ideal size for making fruit cobblers. Sweetened and spiced fresh peaches, apricots or apples or a 30-oz. can of cherries brought from home will combine with a simple biscuit mix crust for a dessert that tastes good hot or cold.

1–1½ quarts fresh peaches, peeled and sliced
1 tablespoon margarine
½ cup water
¾ cup granulated sugar
¼ cup brown sugar
½ teaspoon salt
¼ teaspoon ground cinnamon
2 tablespoons instant tapioca
2 cups biscuit mix, plus ½ cup
2 tablespoons granulated sugar
⅓ cup dry milk powder
¼ cup vegetable shortening
⅔ cup water

Place the sliced peaches in the Dutch oven and dot with the margarine. Add the water. In a small cup, mix the sugars, salt and cinnamon. Add the sugars and spice to the peaches and toss to coat the peaches. Sprinkle the tapioca over the fruit.

In a small bowl, add the dry milk powder and granulated sugar to the biscuit mix. Cut the shortening into the mix with a knife. Add the water and stir until the mixture holds together and pulls away from the side of the bowl. Put this dough on a piece of foil or waxed paper, on which you have spread the ½ cup biscuit mix. Knead the dough, working in the dry mix. Pat the dough into a circle big enough to fit onto the fruit filled Dutch oven. Place the dough carefully over the fruit filling.

Cut some slits on the crust to allow the steam to escape. Place the Dutch oven over 8–10 hot briquets and place 20–25 hot briquets on the flat lid. Cook this cobbler for 15–20 minutes, adding hot coals to the lid as the briquets turn to ash. Remove the pan from the coals. Carefully remove the lid, pulling it straight up and away from the pan, slowly. You don't want any ash on the cobbler. The crust should be brown on the top.* If the crust has not browned, replace the lid, coals intact, and allow the cobbler to cook a little longer. The fruit will be cooked, so no fire under the oven is required. Let the cobbler cool down a bit, then spoon it onto plates or into cups.

*Cooking time depends a lot on weather and wind conditions. The recipe time was determined on a warm, muggy day with a 10 mile-per-hour wind.

FRESH PEACHES WITH HONEY AND LIME

> 3 large ripe peaches
> 6 tablespoons of honey
> fresh limes

Peel the peaches and cut them into halves. Remove the pits. Place the peach halves on plates. Pour a tablespoon of honey into each of the hollows in the peach halves. Sprinkle each peach half with lime juice.

PUDDING AND FRUIT PARFAIT

  2 packages instant vanilla pudding
  1½ cups of canned mixed fruit
  4 cups of milk

Make the pudding according to the package directions. If a shaker is required, use a plastic juice dispenser. Set the pudding in the camp cooler until serving time.

When you are ready for dessert, open and drain the fruit. (Save any juice to add to packaged dry fruit-drink mixes.) Spoon ¼ cup of the pudding into each of 8 paper or plastic cups. Top it with 2 heaping tablespoons of fruit, then with another layer of pudding. Top each portion with an additional tablespoon of fruit, and serve the desserts.

APPLESAUCE CRISP

  1 jar or can (16 ounces) of applesauce
  ½ cup brown sugar
  ½ cup raisins
  1 cup biscuit mix
  ¼ cup softened margarine
  ¼ cup walnuts, almonds or pecans

The liquid for this recipe is in the applesauce. The recipe can be used with an ironware skillet with a tight-fitting lid.

Pour the applesauce into the skillet. Stir in the brown sugar and raisins. Combine the biscuit mix with the softened margarine until the mixture is crumbly. Add the nuts and spread them over the applesauce mixture. Heat over a low flame for 35 or 40 minutes until the top is crispy brown.

CHOCOLATE FONDUE

3 tablespoons margarine
2 tablespoons water or milk (add more if the sauce seems too thick)
2 cups chocolate frosting mix
pinch of ground cinnamon

Melt the margarine in a small saucepan over the camp stove. Add the milk or water and then the dry frosting mix and cinnamon. Mix the sauce thoroughly with a wooden spoon and continue to heat it until it is hot. Let everyone spear a piece of fruit, a marshmallow or piece of cake with his or her own fork and dunk it into the hot chocolate sauce. Better have paper napkins or paper towels ready because a lot of dripping goes on. Chocolate fondue from a common pot is a great ice breaker if you want to invite neighboring campers.

APPENDIX A

▲▲

Menu Plan for a Four-Day Trip for Four Campers

DAY 1

Breakfast
Bloated Oaties
Dry milk powder, for cereal
Tang, to make one quart
Tea or coffee
(Wt. 15 oz. with tea; 16¼ oz. with
   coffee)

Lunch
Trapper's Oat Bread
Honey
Peanut butter
Tang, to make one quart
(Wt. 24½ oz.)

Dinner
Cup of instant chicken vegetable
   soup
Beef, Stroganoff Style
Tofu (optional)

Butterscotch pudding with crumbled
  toffee chips
Tea or coffee or milk
(Wt. 42½ oz. with tofu; 31½ oz.
  without tofu)

Snacks
Trail Mix, ½ cup per hiker
(Wt. 10 oz.)

DAY 2

Breakfast
Bran Muffins, 2 each
Hot cocoa
Tang, to make one quart
(Wt. 33 oz.)

Lunch
Trapper's Oat Bread
Honey
Peanut butter
Tang
Fruit Rolls
(Wt. 31½ oz.)

Dinner
Cup of instant potato soup
Chicken and Chicken Flavored
  Noodle Dinner

Kool Aid, lemon or strawberry
Clothes Pin Biscuit Ring
Chocolate pudding
Coffee
(Wt. 45 oz.)

Snacks
Trail Mix, ½ cup per hiker
(Wt. 10 oz.)

DAY 3

Breakfast
Ham and Potato Patties
Tang, to make one quart
Coffee or tea
(Wt. with tea 15¾ oz.; with coffee
    16½ oz.)

Lunch
Best Guide's Trail Bread
Honey
Peanut butter
Tang, to make one quart
(Wt. 24½ oz.)

Dinner
Asparagus Cheese Soup (omit the
    ham)
Chicken and Potatoes with
    Mushroom Gravy
Cheese cake
Coffee
(Wt. 43 oz.)

Snacks
Trail Mix, ½ cup per hiker
(Wt. 10 oz.)

DAY 4

Breakfast
Bloated Oaties
Dry milk for cereal
Tang, to make one quart
Tea or coffee
(Wt. with tea 15 oz.; with coffee 16¼
    oz.)

Lunch
Trapper's Oat Bread
Honey
Peanut butter
Tang, to make one quart
(Wt. 24½ oz.)

Dinner
Cup of instant split pea soup
Scalloped Potatoes and Ham with
    Cheese Sauce
Chocolate Pudding with Coconut
Spice Tea or coffee
(Wt. 29 oz.)

Snacks
Trail Mix, ½ cup per hiker
(Wt. 10 oz.)

APPENDIX B

▲▲▲▲▲▲▲▲▲▲▲▲▲▲▲▲▲▲▲▲▲▲▲▲▲▲▲▲▲▲▲▲▲▲▲▲▲▲

Weighing It All Up

Use this list as a guide for your own weight and price comparisons. Often, but not always, you can trade money for convenience and lighter weight. Trail food companies often assemble lighter meals than those suggested here, and you don't have to repack the food for the trail. The trash you carry out will weigh less also. For these advantages you will pay a premium.

If your party of four is willing to repack food and carry about two extra pounds apiece, you will save about 45% and have meals that taste closer to those you eat at home. Apply the money you save to the purchase of lightweight, permanent equipment and travel lighter every time you go out.

INGREDIENT WEIGHTS FOR MENU ITEMS (IN OUNCES)

	15¾
Beef, 1 can	14½
Best Guide's Bread	32
Biscuit mix (1¾ cups)	8
Bloated Oaties (2 meals)	12
Bran Muffins (8)	24

Cheese cake	12
Chicken (4 cans)	33
Cocoa mix (2 meals)	9
Coconut/almond toffee chips	6
Coffee (to make four 8-oz. pots)	5
Dry milk powder (4 cups dry)	10
Gravy (dry mix in foil pouches)	2
Ham (2 cans)	13½
Honey (four 8-oz. containers)	40
Herb Mix	1
Kool Aid (to make 2 quarts)	6
Margarine (8 oz. in squeeze bottle)	10
Peanut butter (four ½-cup servings)	20
Pepper	½
Potatoes, noodles, rice	31
Puddings, Pudding and Fruit Rolls	16
Seasoning salt (2 tablespoons)	½
Soups (dry mixes for 4 days)	15¾
Spice Tea Mix	3
Tang	18
Tea bags (16 to make 32 cups)	2
Tofu, Mari Nu brand	11
Trail Mix (2 cups per person)	42
Trapper's Oat Bread (8 pieces)	32
Utensils (cook spoon, wire whisk, measuring cups and spoons, can opener, spatula, knife, clothes pins, aluminum pie pans)	9
Vegetable shortening	4

Total Wt. Four Day Menu and options about 27 pounds. (The trash you pack out will weigh about a pound.)

APPENDIX C

▲▲▲▲▲▲▲▲▲▲▲▲▲▲▲▲▲▲▲▲▲▲▲▲▲▲▲▲▲▲▲▲▲▲▲▲▲▲▲

Shopping List

All items on this list apply to the four-day menu in Appendix A.

MAKE AT HOME RECIPES

5 lbs. unbleached white flour
1 1 lb. box wheat flour
1 1 lb. package brown sugar
1 25.6 oz. box dry milk powder
1 12 oz. jar honey
1 24 oz. bottle safflower oil
2 24 oz. cannisters raisins
3 8 oz. packages pecans
1 8 oz. package chopped dates
½ doz. eggs
¼ or 1 oz. packet cinnamon
2 4 oz. packages walnuts
1 42 oz. box oatmeal
1 12 oz. jar wheat germ
1 6 oz. package dried apples
1 16 oz. can cashew nuts
1 16 oz. can peanuts
2 6 oz. packages mixed dried fruit
1 8 oz. package sunflower kernels

1 16 oz. package candy-coated chocolate bits

1 3½ oz. can shredded coconut

1 roll aluminum foil

1 box 50 resealable plastic bags (sandwich size)

1 box 25 resealable plastic bags (1 gal. size)

Ingredients for herb mix:
    oregano
    basil
    sesame seeds
    thyme
    rosemary
    garlic powder

(All available in ¼-to-1 oz. plastic packets)

1 18 oz. jar peanut butter

1 2.87 oz. jar seasoning salt

1 1 oz. can black pepper

Choice of coffee, instant tea or tea bags

FOR TRAIL RECIPES

4 8″ aluminum pie pans

1 package snap-style clothespins

1 12 oz. can steam-roasted beef

1 5.5 oz. package biscuit mix

1 package complete cheese cake mix

4 6¾ oz. cans boned chicken in broth

1 12 oz. box Swiss Miss hot chocolate mix
1 6 oz. package almond toffee chips
1 25.6 oz. box dry milk powder
1 .87 oz. envelope mushroom gravy mix
1 .87 oz. envelope chicken gravy mix
2 6¾ oz. cans ham chunks
4 8 oz. plastic containers honey
1 6 oz. envelope pre-sweetened powdered drink mix
1 8 oz. squeeze bottle margarine
2 3.8 oz. packages freeze-dried scalloped potatoes
2 3.5 oz. packages freeze-dried chicken-and-mushroom flavored potatoes
1 2 oz. package Borden's Country Store mashed potatoes
1 12 oz. package dry noodles, ½" wide
1 4.3 oz. package freeze-dried stroganoff noodles
1 4.5 oz. package butter-flavored noodles and sauce
1 4 oz. package butterscotch pudding
2 4 oz. packages chocolate pudding
1 4 oz. package fruit rolls
1 4 oz. package pudding rolls
2 2.6 oz. boxes Knorr potato soup
1 2.4 oz. package Knorr split pea soup

1 1.6 oz. package Knorr asparagus
 soup
2 1.2 oz. packages cheese sauce mix
1 6 oz. can shredded coconut
1 4 oz. package butter crystals
1 lb. vegetable shortening sticks
1 10.5 oz. package Mori Nu tofu
 (optional)
1 box cream of chicken instant soup
 packets (only two packets are
 required for trail recipes)
Don't forget stove fuel, weather-
 proofed matches

Index